D0574691

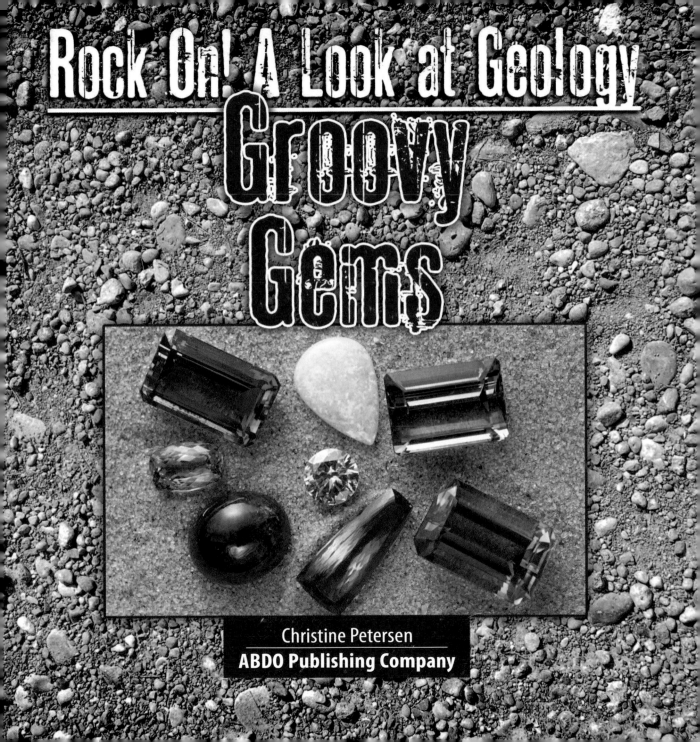

Rock On! A Look at Geology

Groovy Gems

Christine Petersen
ABDO Publishing Company

visit us at
www.abdopublishing.com

Published by ABDO Publishing Company, 8000 West 78th Street, Edina, Minnesota 55439.
Copyright © 2010 by Abdo Consulting Group, Inc. International copyrights reserved in all countries.
No part of this book may be reproduced in any form without written permission from the publisher.
The Checkerboard Library™ is a trademark and logo of ABDO Publishing Company.

Printed in the United States of America, North Mankato, Minnesota.
092009
012010

 PRINTED ON RECYCLED PAPER

Cover Photo: Getty Images
Interior Photos: Alamy pp. 10–11, 21, 22, 26–27; Corbis p. 17; Getty Images pp. 1, 6, 7, 26, 28;
        iStockphoto pp. 5, 7, 8, 9, 12, 17, 21, 23, 24, 25, 29; Peter Arnold pp. 14–15, 22;
        Photo Researchers pp. 15, 16, 24; Photolibrary p. 20; The University of Arizona Herbarium p. 4

Series Coordinator: Megan M. Gunderson
Editors: Heidi M.D. Elston, Megan M. Gunderson
Art Direction & Cover Design: Neil Klinepier

Library of Congress Cataloging-in-Publication Data

Petersen, Christine.
  Groovy gems / Christine Petersen.
        p. cm. -- (Rock on! A look at geology)
  Includes index.
  ISBN 978-1-60453-743-7
  1. Gems--Juvenile literature. 2. Precious stones--Juvenile literature. I. Title.
  QE392.2.P48 2010
  553.8--dc22
                        2009027728

Contents

Erasmus's Lucky Pebble

Erasmus Jacobs didn't know he would change the world. He was just a teenage farm boy living in South Africa. On a summer day in 1866, Erasmus was out on his father's farm. Along the south bank of the Orange River, he found a transparent stone. Erasmus took the stone home.

Not long afterward, a neighbor came to visit the Jacobs farm. His name was Schalk van Niekerk, and he knew a little about

The pebble Erasmus (above) discovered is now known as the Eureka Diamond. His family never received any money from its sale.

geology. When he saw the pebble, he thought it might be a rare mineral. So, Erasmus's mother gave it to him.

Today, diamonds are the most popular gemstone.

Van Niekerk sent the stone to John Robert O'Reilly. O'Reilly identified the stone as a diamond. He then sent the diamond to Dr. William Guybon Atherstone. Atherstone confirmed the stone was a diamond measuring 24 **carats**. That's about the weight of two American pennies.

Erasmus's diamond marked the discovery of diamonds in South Africa. Thousands of miners arrived in South Africa to earn their fortune from diamonds. Since 1866, more than 500 million carats have been mined there. Erasmus and his diamond changed the world of gems!

What Is a Gem?

Walk into any jewelry shop, and you'll see many beautiful gems. Gems such as diamonds are minerals. Pearls are gems, too. Yet these **organic** gems come from animals called mollusks. Amber is a gem that is a fossil. So, what makes all these different substances gems? Gems are materials that humans use for jewelry or decoration. They have three things in common. These are durability,

Star sapphire

rarity, and beauty. They help determine a gem's value.

First, gems need to be durable. They must be able to stand everyday use without scratching or breaking. The hardest gems include rubies, sapphires, and diamonds.

Rarity is another important part of a gem's value. This means it is uncommon. You may never have heard of a gem called benitoite. That is because it is found only in one small part of California.

Lastly, gems are beautiful! Malachite looks like a swirly painting. Some sapphires reflect light in a star shape. White light shining through a diamond may break into a rainbow of colors.

Malachite

North America

Africa

Popular Gems Are Found Worldwide!

South America

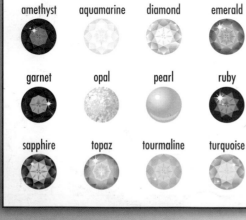

amethyst	aquamarine	diamond	emerald
garnet	opal	pearl	ruby
sapphire	topaz	tourmaline	turquoise

Europe

Asia

Australia

N

W   E

S

Most Gems Are Minerals

Garnet, moonstone, and citrine are well-known gems. They are also minerals. There are more than 3,000 different minerals. But not all minerals are gems. Remember that gems must be durable, rare, and beautiful.

Minerals are the most common solid material found on Earth. Like gems, all minerals share common qualities. First, minerals are formed in nature. They are usually formed by **inorganic** processes.

Like everything on Earth, minerals are built from tiny particles called atoms. Each type of mineral has a specific chemical

A diamond is strong because of the way its carbon atoms are arranged.

makeup. For example, quartz always has two atoms of oxygen for every one atom of silicon.

Some mineral gems contain atoms of just one **element**. Diamond is made of only carbon atoms. Other mineral gems are mixtures of two or more elements. For example, topaz contains five.

Last, a mineral's atoms are arranged in a specific pattern to form solid units called crystals. All crystals of the same mineral have the same basic shape. Some crystals are many feet long, while others can be seen only with a microscope.

Six Crystal Systems

    Each mineral's specific crystal shape comes from the way its atoms are arranged. Scientists have fit all these different shapes into six groups called systems. These are isometric, tetragonal, orthorhombic, hexagonal, monoclinic, and triclinic.

    The simplest isometric crystals are shaped like cubes. Diamond is an isometric gem. The simplest tetragonal crystal form is a **prism**. The

Ruby fits in the hexagonal crystal system.

mineral zircon fits in this system. It can be cut to look like a diamond.

Orthorhombic crystals may have a double pyramid shape. Peridot is a green orthorhombic gem. Hexagonal crystals may look like columns. Beryl is a common hexagonal mineral. Its grass green form is the gem emerald.

The simplest monoclinic crystals resemble rectangular boxes with angled tops and bottoms. Jadeite is a monoclinic mineral that provides green gems. The faces of triclinic crystals do not meet at right angles. Turquoise is a blue or green triclinic gem.

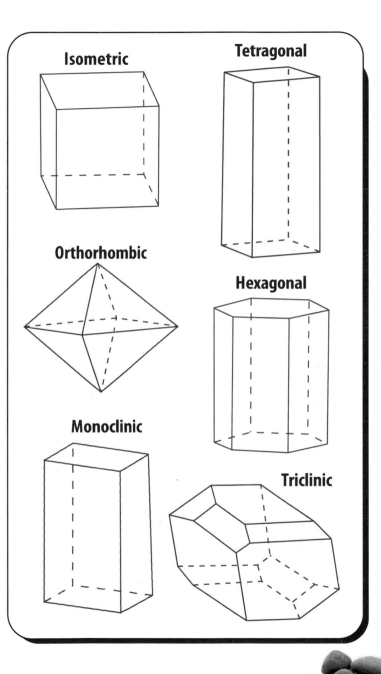

Isometric

Tetragonal

Orthorhombic

Hexagonal

Monoclinic

Triclinic

Magma Gems

Mineral gems need special conditions to form. Some grow from hot liquids that gradually cool down, such as **magma**.

Magma forms in or below Earth's crust and then moves upward toward the surface. It can fill large or small spaces in the crust. Or, it can erupt at the surface as lava. Either way, it then begins cooling.

As magma cools, crystals grow. Slower cooling produces larger crystals. This process can take millions of years. Aquamarine, emerald, topaz, and tourmaline often form this way.

Some gems are simply carried up toward Earth's surface by magma. More than 100 miles (160 km) down, great heat and pressure rearranged carbon into a new crystal structure.

Brazil provides much of the world's aquamarine.

This formed diamonds. Rising **magma** carried these tough crystals nearer to the surface, where we find them today.

Tourmaline can form in many colors, including pink and green watermelon.

Water Gems

Geodes are round like our planet. Their name comes from a Latin word meaning "earthlike."

Some gems form with the help of water. Have you ever seen a geode? It looks like a plain, round rock. The surprise comes when you break it open. The inside is filled with crystals!

Scientists think each geode began as gasses trapped inside rock. Change happened slowly as water flowed around the rock for millions of years. Minerals in the water were deposited inside the rock, where they formed layers of crystals. Amethyst and other quartz crystals are often found inside geodes.

Water also helps form opals. The **element** silica settles out of the water and hardens in cracks between rocks. The tiny **spheres** of silica must be arranged just right. When they are, the opals become swirling, shimmering blocks of color.

Sunlight can cause turquoise gems to fade.

Opals must be protected against drying out. Otherwise, they can form cracks. This is called crazing.

Turquoise also relies on water to form. As mineral-rich water seeps through rock, it deposits the turquoise. Turquoise contains the **element** copper, which gives the gem its blue or green coloring.

Make a Geode!

What You'll Need

- 1 cup water
- medium saucepan
- table salt
- wooden spoon
- food coloring
- egg carton
- clean eggshell

What You'll Do

1. Ask an adult for help!

2. Pour the water into the saucepan. Bring it to a boil on the stove.

3. Add salt to the water until no more will dissolve, stirring constantly.

4. Turn off the stove and add about 3 drops of food coloring.

5. Set the clean eggshell in the egg carton. Pour or spoon the salt mixture into the eggshell. It should reach almost to the very top.

6. Set your experiment in a place where it won't be disturbed. Over the next few days, crystals will form as the water disappears.

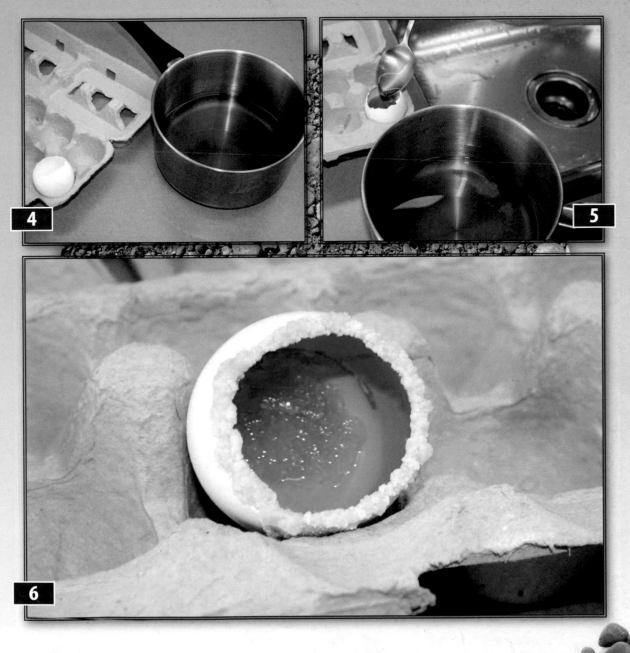

Living Gems

Gem coral grows in places such as the Mediterranean Sea and the Sea of Japan.

Some gems come from living things. People collect these **organic** gems from both land and sea. They include pearl, coral, amber, and jet.

A pearl forms inside a mollusk, such as an oyster. It begins when a small piece of shell or a tiny animal enters the oyster. The oyster forms layers of smooth, shiny material called nacre around the object. This builds the beautiful pearls people use as gems.

Small animals called coral polyps create coral. Coral gems come from those that build an **internal** skeleton. When they die, the skeleton is left behind. It is hard enough to be used in jewelry but soft enough to carve.

Amber and jet are gems that are also fossils. Amber is transparent and yellow to red in color. It is from the **resin** of ancient pine trees. Often, ancient insects and plants are trapped inside amber!

Jet is amber's opposite. It is black in color and quite lightweight. This gem is made of fossilized wood from trees that lived during the time of the dinosaurs.

Amber is found throughout the world. But, much of it is from northern Europe.

Coral is polished to make jewelry.

Imitations and Synthetics

Gems are often expensive to buy. Imitation and synthetic gems solve this problem. They look lovely but cost less.

Imitation gems look like natural gems. But, they do not have the same chemical makeup. They are often made of glass. Glass

Citrine (above) *may be used to imitate topaz* (left).

can be produced in many colors. However, it is not as hard as most gems. And, it may contain bubbles.

Composite gems also imitate the real thing. These combine gems with other materials. Some imitation emeralds are made this way. For example, a composite may be a thin layer of a gem over a layer of glass. Or, a thin layer of green glass may be placed between two layers of colorless quartz.

Other imitation gems are simply one type of gem replacing another. Citrine can look like topaz. Colorless quartz can imitate diamond.

Synthetic gems are grown in laboratories. Unlike imitation gems, they have the same chemical makeup as natural gems. Their crystal structures are also the same. So, it can take an expert to tell the difference between natural and synthetic gems! Emeralds, rubies, and sapphires are a few gems that can be made this way.

PRECIOUS METALS

Like gems, some metals are valued for their beauty and rarity. So, they often serve as settings for gems in jewelry and decoration. These precious metals include gold, silver, platinum, iridium, and palladium.

Cultured Pearls

Cultured pearls may sound as fake as glass emeralds. But they aren't imitation or synthetic! Cultured pearls are natural. They come from a partnership between people and oysters.

Cultured pearls are farmed like a crop. When oyster shells grow to a certain size, a small nacre bead is placed inside each one. The bead works like a seed

Divers tend the oysters as the pearls grow. Nets and cages protect the oysters and their pearls.

When the pearls are ready, they are removed from their shells.

Pearls come in a variety of colors.

from which a pearl grows. The oysters are then placed in underwater nets or cages. This protects the oysters while the pearls grow.

The oysters build pearls much as they would naturally. As the pearls grow, divers care for them. After one to three years, the oysters are opened and the pearls are removed. About 1 in 20 oysters contains a valuable, gem-quality pearl.

Today, most pearls sold in the world are cultured pearls. It is far less expensive to produce cultured pearls than to harvest natural ones. Most cultured pearls are produced in Japan and Australia.

Working with Gems

It takes many careful steps to create a brilliant cut diamond.

It takes a lot to make gems into beautiful pieces of jewelry. Many gems must be mined from within the earth. Pearls and coral are harvested from the sea.

Then, skilled workers cut and polish the gems to create wearable jewels. Gems can be cut in different ways to increase their beauty and value. The cut is chosen to best show off each gem's qualities.

Many gems are cut to have flat faces called facets. The brilliant cut is popular for diamonds. Common cuts also include step cuts, mixed cuts, and fancy cuts.

Other gems look their best when polished or carved instead of given facets. Gems with a cabochon cut are polished in the shape of a dome. This style is popular for turquoise gems.

Moonstone often receives a cabochon cut.

CONFLICT DIAMONDS

Diamonds have been used to finance illegal behavior and wars in some countries. So today, the Kimberley Process aims to prevent the trade of these "conflict diamonds." It carefully regulates the diamond trade by tracking diamonds from mine to market.

Then and Now

Gems have been treasured for thousands of years. Ancient people wore crystals as protection against evil. Gems were buried with the dead for use in the afterlife. Some people even ground up gems and swallowed them to treat illnesses!

Glittering jewels have long been symbols of wealth and power, too. They grace royal crowns and decorate the necks of modern celebrities.

Great Britain's Imperial State Crown holds more than 3,000 gems.

Diamonds are especially popular in jewelry. But this beloved gem has many other uses. That is because diamonds are the hardest natural substance on Earth. More than 75 percent of all diamonds are too small, poorly colored, or flawed to be used in jewelry. Instead, they become industrial diamonds. They are used in tools such as glass cutters and rock drills.

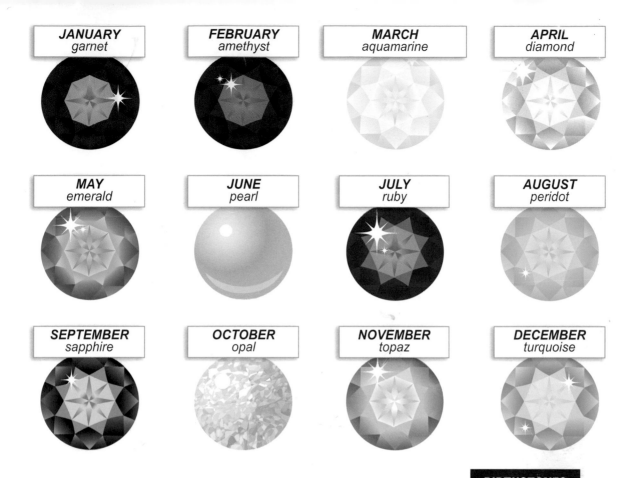

JANUARY garnet	FEBRUARY amethyst	MARCH aquamarine	APRIL diamond
MAY emerald	JUNE pearl	JULY ruby	AUGUST peridot
SEPTEMBER sapphire	OCTOBER opal	NOVEMBER topaz	DECEMBER turquoise

Diamonds are so hard they can only be cut using diamond dust! Ground diamonds are also used to shape other gems, especially sapphires and rubies. However they are used, gems are rare and beautiful natural works of art.

BIRTHSTONES

For thousands of years, people have believed certain gemstones bring good luck and good health. These traditions led to birthstones. Today, each month is assigned at least one gem. Birthstones are said to bring good luck to those born in that month. Which one is yours?

Glossary

carat - a unit of weight for precious stones. It is equal to 200 milligrams.

element - any of the more than 100 simple substances made of atoms of only one kind.

inorganic - being or made of matter other than plant or animal.

internal - of, relating to, or being on the inside.

magma - melted rock beneath Earth's surface.

organic - relating to or coming from living things.

prism - a solid with a top and a bottom joined by at least three sides. The ends are the same size and shape and are parallel.

resin - a sticky, translucent, yellow or brown substance that comes from certain trees.

sphere - a globe-shaped body.

Saying It

amethyst - A-muh-thuhst
benitoite - buh-NEED-uh-wite
cabochon - KA-buh-shahn
malachite - MA-luh-kite
nacre - NAY-kuhr
orthorhombic - awr-thuh-RAHM-bihk
polyp - PAH-luhp
sapphire - SA-fire
sphere - SFIHR
turquoise - TUHR-koyz

Web Sites

To learn more about gems, visit ABDO Publishing Company on the World Wide Web at **www.abdopublishing.com**. Web sites about gems are featured on our Book Links page. These links are routinely monitored and updated to provide the most current information available.

Index